P&

A HISTORY

Ruth Artmonsky

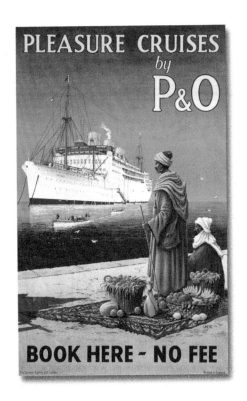

SHIRE PUBLICATIONS

Published by Shire Publications, part of Bloomsbury
Publishing Plc
PO Box 883, Oxford, OX1 9PL, UK
1385 Broadway, 5th Floor, New York, NY 10018, USA
Email: shire@shirebooks.co.uk   www.shirebooks.co.uk

© 2012 The Peninsular and Oriental Steam
Navigation Company.

First published in 2012
Transferred to digital print on demand 2017

A CIP catalogue record for this book is available from the
British Library.

Shire Library no. 701.   ISBN-13: 978 0 74781 170 1

Ruth Artmonsky has asserted her right under the
Copyright, Designs and Patents Act, 1988, to be identified
as the author of this book.

Designed by Tony Truscott Designs, Sussex, UK
Typeset in Perpetua and Gill Sans.
Printed and bound in Great Britain.

COVER IMAGE
Detail from a P&O poster advertising post-war cruises,
designed for the company by John Gilroy.

TITLE PAGE IMAGE
One of a series of 1930s posters advertising cruises
on P&O's luxury liners known as the 'Straths' or 'The
White Sisters'.

CONTENTS PAGE IMAGE
Wood engraving used to illustrate P&O's information
leaflets in the 1950s.

ACKNOWLEDGEMENTS
The major resource for the book has been the P&O
Heritage Collection. My thanks are to Susie Cox, the
Collection's Curator, and her colleagues, Beth Ellis,
Anna-Klara Hahn and Cori Convertito-Farrar, for the
exceptional interest they have taken in compiling the
book and the professional help they have so generously
provided.

All P&O images are reproduced by kind permission of
the P&O Heritage Collection. Other illustrations are
acknowledged as follows:
Assisted passage card on page 60, by kind permission of
the People's History Museum; Spirit of Britain image,
page 61, by kind permission of P&O Ferries.

P&O HERITAGE
P&O Heritage exists to preserve the maritime history and
collections of P&O and is proudly supported by DP World,
who acquired the P&O company in 2006.
www.poheritage.com

CONTENTS

DELIVERING THE MAIL

IN 1863 A P&O PASSENGER, Mrs Dulcimer, wrote to a friend:

> If you are ever shipwrecked, my dearest Laura, do contrive to get the
> catastrophe conducted by the Peninsular and Oriental Company. I believe
> other companies drown you sometimes, and drowning is a very prosaic
> arrangement ... fit only for sea-faring people and second class passengers.
> I have just been shipwrecked under the auspices of P&O and I assure you that
> it is the pleasantest thing imaginable. It had its little hardships, to be sure, but
> so has a picnic, and the wreck was one of the most agreeable picnics you can
> imagine.

It was P&O's reliability, in the most extreme circumstances, that not only
endeared it to ladies in distress but also made it attractive to the British
government, and in particular to the Admiralty. It was the Admiralty's
recognition of the potential trustworthiness of a small but ambitious shipping
company, trading modestly between England and Spain and Portugal (the
Peninsula), that led to it being entrusted to carry the Royal Mail overseas.
Such was the humble start of P&O, which was to grow into one of the largest
shipping companies, dominating the routes from England to the Middle and
Far East for well over a century. Without the mail contract this might well
never have happened.

Brodie McGhie Willcox set up a shipbroking and insurance partnership
with a Mr Carreno soon after the end of the Napoleonic Wars. Little is known
of Carreno, although his name suggests a connection with the Iberian
Peninsula, which was to be the destination for their initial shipping ventures.
What proved to be their first momentous decision in 1815 was to take on a
young unemployed naval clerk, Arthur Anderson. Anderson was introduced
to Willcox by Christopher Hill, a Scarborough ship owner, and later his
father-in-law. As with many rags-to-riches stories, possibly embellished,
Anderson is described as having been a poor Shetland 'beach boy', earning
his living at the tender age of eleven by curing fish.

Opposite:
Watercolour of a
P&O mail steamer
at Brindisi, Italy.
The company ran
a mail service from
Brindisi to
Alexandria from
1870 to 1914.
British
Government mail
contracts were
essential to the
foundation and
early success of
P&O. (Painted by
William Whitelock
Lloyd, c. 1880s–
1890s.)

5

Portrait of Brodie McGhie Willcox. Born in 1786, Willcox followed his ship-owning uncle to London and set up a ship broking business in 1815. Willcox served as joint Managing Director and later Chairman of P&O until his death in 1862.

Arthur Anderson joined Willcox as a young shipping clerk and quickly became his partner in Willcox & Anderson and later the Peninsular Steam Navigation Company. Anderson was joint Managing Director and succeeded Willcox as Chairman of P&O.

Captain Richard Bourne was born in 1770 into a reputable Dublin family, joining his brothers in business after a career in the Royal Navy. Bourne and his business associates were instrumental in P&O's success. (All three portraits of P&O's founding fathers were painted in oils by Thomas Francis Dicksee in 1850.)

Whether by intent or not, Anderson's arrival was significant. When Carreno retired in 1823 Anderson replaced him and the partnership changed to Willcox and Anderson. Within a dozen years the firm had grown from a small shipping company, chartering ships to and from the Peninsula as and when opportunities presented themselves, to one running a regular steamship service under the splendid name 'The Peninsular Steam Navigation Company'.

The first ship regularly plying the Peninsula route for the company was the *William Fawcett*, a wooden paddle steamer chartered from The Dublin & London Steam Packet Company of whom Captain Richard Bourne RN was a director. Bourne met Willcox & Anderson in 1834 and was to play a pivotal part in the P&O story. Once described as one of the 'most important men' in his native country of Ireland, Bourne was well connected and at sixty-four he combined age and experience both in steam navigation and winning mail contracts. Together with his associates, including Charles Wye Williams, Bourne appreciated the potential of the Peninsula run, and brought ships and investors to The Peninsular Steam Navigation Company. Willcox, Anderson and now Bourne were to form a team that combined accounting frugality with experience, entrepreneurial imagination and risk taking. But it was Bourne who, on behalf of the company, negotiated and signed the significant contract with the Admiralty in 1837 to run a regular mail service from Falmouth to Spain and Portugal, putting in at Vigo, Oporto, Lisbon, Cadiz and Gibraltar. The departure of the first contract mail sailing, on 4 September 1837 from Falmouth, is traditionally accepted as the true foundation of P&O.

William Fawcett was chartered from Captain Richard Bourne and is generally regarded as the first steamer to run on the company's fledgling Peninsula service. The ship was launched in 1829 and named after the man who built her engines. In this later painting she is shown with HMS *Queen*, in what might be a fictional encounter. (Detail from a painting by Frank Stewart Murray, 1893.)

The earliest P&O mail vessels were: *Don Juan*, *Tagus*, *Braganza*, *Liverpool* (all owned by Bourne) and *Iberia* – the first vessel built entirely to the order of Willcox and Anderson. Together the Peninsular Steam Navigation Company fleet flew the P&O flag, displaying its Peninsula origins: blue and white for the House of Braganza and red and gold (yellow) for the Spanish Bourbons.

The first mail run was on the *Don Juan* which, along with the *Braganza*, was advertised as the 'largest and most powerful ship yet afloat.' For the *Don Juan*, her first voyage was also to be her last as she ran aground in the fog at the southernmost tip of the Peninsula on the homeward run. Among the passengers on board were Arthur Anderson and his wife, and history would have it that Anderson not only got a messenger to take news of the mishap overland to Gibraltar, but also negotiated with local fishermen to take him, with his wife, the mail and the mail's minder back to Gibraltar by sea. Anderson understood his priorities – the mail had precedence and any lateness would incur penalties.

The Admiralty insisted that the mail should always be accompanied by its representative, usually a retired naval officer, who had the authority to

Plan of the
wooden paddle
steamer *Iberia*, the
first vessel built
entirely to the
order and pocket
of Willcox and
Anderson in 1836.
P&O's founders
were great
believers in the
possibilities of
steam navigation
over sail.

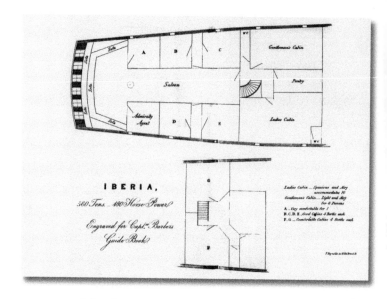

Lieutenant Bundy,
resplendent in
his naval uniform,
depicted
accompanying the
Royal Mail going
ashore at Vigo.
(Woodcut after
a drawing by
Thackeray,
published in
*Cornhill to Grand
Cairo* in 1846.)

countermand the ship's captain, if anything arose that might affect the schedule. Inevitably there were spats. One such 'minder' was described as 'an old red-faced man, very fond of his grog and particularly great in his own importance.' Thackeray's description of Lieutenant Bundy, the guardian of Her Majesty's mail on a P&O voyage he took in 1844, was altogether more generous:

... issuing from his cabin in his long swallow-tailed coat with anchor buttons; his sabre clattering between his legs, a magnificent shirt collar of several inches in height around his good-humoured, sallow face; and above it a cocked hat that shone so I thought it was made of polished tin ...

By 1840 P&O was carrying mail beyond Gibraltar, across the Mediterranean to Alexandria: the first ship to run the route being the *Oriental*. Along with the mail the ships would carry a certain number of passengers and precious freight, including bullion. The fleet was 'puffed' as having construction and machinery 'of tried improvement adopted without regard to expense. In the planning and layout of the accommodation the comfort and convenience of passengers have been studiously kept in view.'

Such claims rarely mentioned the reality of the weather or, indeed, of the fellow 'travellers' kept below deck. Mr L. M. Wood, who travelled to Alexandria on the *Oriental* in 1846, wrote of the chaotic scene on the ship's departure:

passengers crying and lamenting on leaving their friends and relatives, some hunting for their luggage without effect, pigs grunting, calves bellowing, cocks crowing, geese screaming, crew drunk, officers swearing, steam blowing off ...

A watercolour of Gibraltar painted in 1846 by the artist, Andrew Nicholl, from a P&O steamer. With short stops at Lisbon and Cadiz, P&O's peninsula mail steamers could reach Gibraltar in seven days.

Before the invention of stabilisers there was little that could be done to lessen the discomfort of heavy seas. Only the most stalwart remained on deck as P&O's *Zambesi* crossed the Bay of Biscay in 1875. (Engraving from *The Graphic*.)

Below deck many were confined to cabins, incapacitated with sea sickness. For the lucky few still standing, the continual rolling and pitching, or the roughs and 'smooths' as W.W. Lloyd described them, made dressing for dinner particularly hazardous. (Lithograph from *P&O Pencillings* by W.W. Lloyd.)

Without refrigeration animals were shipped alive and, along with their noise and smells, there was the incessant sound of the blacksmith's anvil and the throb of the engines. And then there was the weather, particularly crossing the Bay of Biscay. Paddle steamers had a tendency to roll from side to side and to pitch, lifting the paddles out of the water, which could stop the engines. An 1854 diary described the hazards of dressing in heavy seas:

> First I bumped my head against the top of my berth while putting my stockings on – then on descending to the floor to put on my trousers I was pitched head first into my companion's bed, and, finally, after having washed, I was suddenly capsized amongst a heap of trunks.

With the extension of the mail service across the Mediterranean the word 'Oriental' was added to The Peninsular Steam Navigation Company name, thenceforth familiarly to be abbreviated to P&O. It was as The Peninsular and Oriental Steam Navigation Company that P&O was incorporated by Royal Charter in 1840. The original Egyptian mail contract had stipulated that a mail service to India should be established within two years and, complying with this, the company became even more 'Oriental', extending its service to India and Ceylon, and later to Singapore, Hong Kong and Australasia.

There was just the small problem to tackle of how to carry the mail safely over some 150 miles of desert from the Mediterranean to the Red Sea: from Alexandria to Suez. As early as 1829 a pioneering chancer, Lieutenant Thomas Waghorn, had started a courier service over much of this route and by the 1830s was running a regular service for letters and parcels entrusted to him. Waghorn soon had a competitor, J. R. Hill, both men making arrangements for camel trains to carry the mail and for rather basic rest houses en route. It has been estimated that at one time some four thousand camels were carrying mail, luggage and freight. Passengers were transported by an altogether slower route: starting with horse-drawn barges on the Mahmoudie Canal; then vermin-ridden steamers down the Nile; and finally in horse-drawn six-seater wagons from Cairo to Suez.

It was the spirited Anderson who was sent out to get some sort of rationalisation to the desert crossing. He managed to get Waghorn and Hill to combine forces, had steam tugs to replace horses and even organised the building of a lock to raise the canal barges on to the Nile. New Nile steamers were commissioned – the *Lotus* and the *Cairo* – with berths for passengers; and better tariffs were renegotiated with the Pasha, who virtually controlled the desert routes. It was vital for P&O to ensure the reliable transit of the mails and, indeed, to uphold their reputation, which was in danger of being tainted by the misapprehension that the arrangements of Waghorn and Hill were actually P&O's.

Watercolour of the frontispiece to *The Route of the Overland Mail to India*, published in 1851 as an illustrated account of the passage of the Indian mail from Southampton to Calcutta.

Sorting the mail in the 'post office' on board the P&O steamer *Pekin* was hot work in the Red Sea. (Engraving published in *The Graphic* in 1875.)

By 1856 the new Egyptian railway from Alexandria had reached Cairo and, in 1858, a senior Post Office official, the novelist Anthony Trollope, was sent out to further improve transit arrangements from Cairo. It was Trollope who negotiated with the Egyptian government to carry the mail on the recently completed rail link to Suez.

For the journey on from Suez to India it was necessary to have bigger and more powerful ships, capable of withstanding the monsoons, and P&O's *Hindostan* and the *Bentinck* were launched in 1842 and 1843 respectively. These were still wooden paddle steamers, carrying some 150 passengers (specified as 102 passengers and fifty servants) and advertised as superb, magnificent, and commodious. P&O was enabled to develop its fleet because of the mail subsidy that facilitated an all-year-round service in spite of passenger numbers dipping during the monsoon season.

The historic departure from Southampton of P&O's *Hindostan* in 1842. Specially commissioned for mail service from Suez to India, *Hindostan* was the company's largest and most luxurious steamer. (Painted by R. H. Neville-Cumming.)

At Aden the mails were conveyed on specially constructed trucks 'under the watchful eye of an European official'. (*P&O Sketches in Pen & Ink* by Harry Furniss, c. 1890s.)

By the late 1850s P&O was running weekly mail services to the Peninsula, twice monthly to India and China and every two months to Singapore and Sydney. The handling of the mail had been systematised – space and storage plans had to be worked out for each trip in advance, approved by the captain, and forwarded to the Admiralty. Each mail bag was tagged for its destination: Port Said and the Middle East with a grey tag; Aden and East Africa with pink; Bombay buff; Ceylon red and white; and so on.

Eventually the mail from England was sent down to Marseilles by train where it would be loaded on to a P&O ship arriving from Gibraltar. Loading usually took place at night and with at times nearly a thousand bags, it could take up to five hours. Loading and unloading times became something of a competition. The Bombay Post Office once boasted that they could unload the mail within two hours of a steamer rounding its lighthouse.

The P&O mail steamer service was considered one of the wonders of its day. A regular, reliable service was not only essential for commercial reasons, but as a lifeline for British nationals working overseas, often in quite solitary conditions. For P&O passengers it provided an opportunity to keep in touch with loved ones en route. Well into the twentieth century diaries and letters home were punctuated with the expressed need to break off so that a letter could catch the mail at the next port of call.

Letter carried on a P&O steamer from Sydney to Bombay in 1872, a journey of one month, before being transported overland to Calcutta.

P&O and BRITISH INDIA S.N.Cos'

Total Fleet Tonnage 1,154,769 Tons.

COLOMBO HARBOUR

PASSENGER SERVICES

**MEDITERRANEAN
EGYPT INDIA
PERSIAN GULF
BURMA STRAITS**

**CHINA JAPAN
AUSTRALASIA
EAST&SOUTH AFRICA
MAURITIUS &c &c**

QUIS SEPARABIT

1917

JANUARY
SUN		7	14	21	28
MON	1	8	15	22	29
TUE	2	9	16	23	30
WED	3	10	17	24	31
THU	4	11	18	25	
FRI	5	12	19	26	
SAT	6	13	20	27	

FEBRUARY
SUN		4	11	18	25
MON		5	12	19	26
TUE		6	13	20	27
WED		7	14	21	28
THU	1	8	15	22	
FRI	2	9	16	23	
SAT	3	10	17	24	

MARCH
SUN		4	11	18	25
MON		5	12	19	26
TUE		6	13	20	27
WED		7	14	21	28
THU	1	8	15	22	29
FRI	2	9	16	23	30
SAT	3	10	17	24	31

APRIL
SUN	1	8	15	22	29
MON	2	9	16	23	30
TUE	3	10	17	24	
WED	4	11	18	25	
THU	5	12	19	26	
FRI	6	13	20	27	
SAT	7	14	21	28	

MAY
SUN		6	13	20	27
MON		7	14	21	28
TUE	1	8	15	22	29
WED	2	9	16	23	30
THU	3	10	17	24	31
FRI	4	11	18	25	
SAT	5	12	19	26	

JUNE
SUN		3	10	17	24
MON		4	11	18	25
TUE		5	12	19	26
WED		6	13	20	27
THU		7	14	21	28
FRI	1	8	15	22	29
SAT	2	9	16	23	30

EUROPE ASIA
P&O route B.I. routes
EGYPT CHINA JAPAN
AFRICA NORTH PACIFIC OCEAN
INDIAN OCEAN
SOUTH ATLANTIC OCEAN AUSTRALIA

1917

JULY
SUN	1	8	15	22	29
MON	2	9	16	23	30
TUE	3	10	17	24	31
WED	4	11	18	25	
THU	5	12	19	26	
FRI	6	13	20	27	
SAT	7	14	21	28	

AUGUST
SUN		5	12	19	26
MON		6	13	20	27
TUE		7	14	21	28
WED	1	8	15	22	29
THU	2	9	16	23	30
FRI	3	10	17	24	31
SAT	4	11	18	25	

SEPTEMBER
SUN		2	9	16	23	30
MON		3	10	17	24	
TUE		4	11	18	25	
WED		5	12	19	26	
THU		6	13	20	27	
FRI		7	14	21	28	
SAT	1	8	15	22	29	

OCTOBER
SUN		7	14	21	28
MON	1	8	15	22	29
TUE	2	9	16	23	30
WED	3	10	17	24	31
THU	4	11	18	25	
FRI	5	12	19	26	
SAT	6	13	20	27	

NOVEMBER
SUN		4	11	18	25
MON		5	12	19	26
TUE		6	13	20	27
WED		7	14	21	28
THU	1	8	15	22	29
FRI	2	9	16	23	30
SAT	3	10	17	24	

DECEMBER
SUN		2	9	16	23	30
MON		3	10	17	24	31
TUE		4	11	18	25	
WED		5	12	19	26	
THU		6	13	20	27	
FRI		7	14	21	28	
SAT	1	8	15	22	29	

Head Offices
LONDON

PENINSULAR & ORIENTAL STEAM NAVIGATION C?
122 LEADENHALL S? E.C. & 17 NORTHUMBERLAND AV. W.C. ‡ **BRITISH INDIA STEAM NAVIGATION COMPANY**
17 NORTHUMBERLAND AV. W.C. & GRAY, DAWES & C? 25 G? WINCHESTER S? E.C.

SERVING THE EMPIRE

P&O NEEDED THE MAIL CONTRACTS and it needed the Empire, for as long as the Empire thrived there would always be mail and passengers to transport to and from it. A veteran traveller, writing in 1913, illustrated how closely the public saw the connection: 'Every British and Imperialist is proud of The Peninsular and Oriental Navigation Company. We feel it is part of the British Constitution.' The majority of P&O passengers in the nineteenth century were British. Typical were a group of Bombay to Suez travellers observed by Thackeray at a Cairo staging post: 'Thirty Indian officers in moustaches and jackets; ten civilians in ditto and spectacles; ten pale-faced ladies with ringlets, to whom all paid prodigious attention.'

India was a major destination for both mail and passengers; not only for the army and for the colonial service, but for planters, traders, missionaries, doctors and, from time to time, big game hunters. Many were variously accompanied by wives and children, batmen and servants, maids and nannies. P&O carried clergymen of a variety of persuasions who were taking their particular 'word' far afield. It also carried pilgrims to the Holy Land and, in time, would play a major part in transporting Muslim pilgrims from Pakistan and East Africa to Jedda, the closest port for Mecca.

And then there was the 'fishing fleet', as one observer put it, 'trailing their crêpe de Chine sails for Colombo and points North.' These were young ladies seeking husbands, some, it was rumoured, so optimistic as to have their trousseau with them. One young girl writing home complained of the 'suet pudding' of a young man she had been placed next to at table. However, once she had started on her campaign in earnest, she was able to report: 'Already I've spoken to more men in ten days than possible during six weeks or even six months in Southboro!'

On any voyage a pecking order would emerge similar to that in life ashore. Generals and senior administrators considered themselves top of the first-class tree and tended to have their own coterie around them. Second-class passengers were equally sensitive as to who could be considered acceptable, or not: 'Among the Second Class passengers there was not one who could legitimately be called

Opposite:
Calendar for 1917 jointly advertising P&O and British India's regular services which, in spite of the war, the company maintained.

15

Long voyages east gave single ladies ample opportunity to catch a potential husband en route and earned them the nickname, the 'fishing fleet'. (Lithograph from *P&O Pencillings* by W. W. Lloyd.)

a bounder, nor was there one who, in its objectionable sense, could properly be called a cad.'

P&O officers and crews were similarly hierarchical. In the Victorian period the majority of the captains (commanders in P&O parlance) were drawn from the Royal Navy and rank and discipline followed naval traditions. In addition to the captain there were commonly four or five officers, a purser and a chief engineer. Besides British ratings there would be Lascars from Indian coastal regions and engine 'boys' from East Africa.

P&O ships carried all manner of passengers travelling to and from the Empire for business or pleasure. Many of these were acutely observed and caricatured by W. W. Lloyd and published in *P&O Pencillings* in 1892.

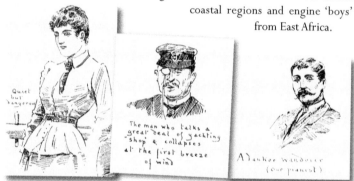

London replaced Southampton as the company's home port in 1874. Departures and arrivals of particular persons of note on P&O ships were regularly reported in the Court Circular of *The Times* newspaper. (Lithograph from *P&O Pencillings* by W. W. Lloyd)

A P&O Commander photographed with his Senior Deck Officers in 1910. P&O uniforms, like the company's early captains and officers, were drawn from the Royal Navy and followed naval conventions.

P&O captains were the absolute monarchs of their vessels. Before the invention of wireless telegraphy limited means of communication meant that captains made their own decisions (in line with company regulations, of course). As befitted their status, the captains' attire was resplendent and consisted of a blue frock coat, double-breasted, with eight gold buttons on either side. The rank of an officer could be discerned by the amount of gold braid and the number of buttons sported.

In the early days, the chief engineer and his 'boys' were considered rather alien creatures, restricted as to where they could go on board ship by the dirt and grease on their work clothes. In background and training

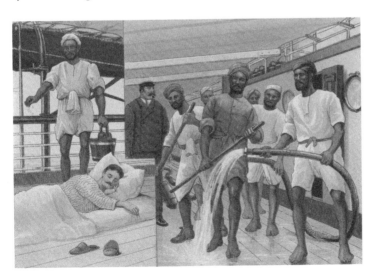

Long before air conditioning the heat of the Red Sea drove many passengers to sleep on deck – running the gauntlet of the 'the morning watch' or wash. (Lithograph from *P&O Pencillings* by W. W. Lloyd.)

17

P&O engineers on board *Massilia* photographed in 1889. In the early days when the demands of mail schedules required 'full speed', the relationship between the Deck and Engine departments was often strained.

the engineers differed from the deck officers too and much was made of the friction that often existed between them (greatly exacerbated by the demands of keeping the mail steamers to schedule and speed). From time to time directives were issued reminding both departments of their obligations: 'A perfect understanding between the commander and the chief engineer is essential to the efficient working of the ship and must be cultivated on both sides.'

The 'engine boys' or stokers were charged with feeding the furnaces. The 'stokehole' was said to recall 'visions of Doré's picture of the Inferno'. (Lithograph from *P&O Pencillings* by W. W. Lloyd)

Over the years P&O had several offices in London including a passenger booking office close to Trafalgar Square. In 1937 the Cockspur Street office was decorated in celebration of the company's centenary and the Coronation of King George VI.

Staff at the Hong Kong office photographed in the 1860s with Thomas Sutherland seated in the centre. Sutherland made his mark in Hong Kong, where he furthered the interests of P&O and founded the Hong Kong & Shanghai Bank.

Before the Suez Canal was built P&O passengers travelling to India and beyond had to endure an arduous journey from Alexandria to Suez involving various modes of transport including horse-drawn carriages said to resemble Brighton bathing boxes.

Rules and regulations abounded and were part of an enormous flow of instructions from London governing all aspects of running the ship down to the proper serving of tea in Rockingham teapots.

Although directed from Head Office in London, P&O officers and crews were supplied locally by P&O depots at established ports of call. The depot and agency staff were responsible for the essential storage and supply of coal, provisions and freight, and administered warehouses, wharfs, workshops, tugs, and even farms and hostelries. As the company's agents they engaged

P&O first arrived in Hong Kong in 1845 and built an office in Kowloon a few years later. Renowned for its elaborate cast-iron balconies the P&O building acquired the nick name 'tit hong' or iron house. (Contemporary watercolour by a Chinese artist.)

commercially and politically with their respective territories and often acted as unofficial representatives of the British government.

The opening of the Suez Canal in 1869 was a key date for the company. Before that, P&O's passengers for India and the Far East would have to disembark at Alexandria and then make the arduous journey across Egypt to Suez where they would re-embark on another P&O vessel. The journey from one ship to another would involve taking small, grubby canal boats with no berths or washing facilities (other than a bucket over the side) on to Nile boats with only two compartments (one for each sex), and then across the desert in horse-drawn vans, said to resemble Brighton bathing boxes. Each van would take six voyagers, sitting knee to knee, four vans travelling as a caravan.

Although the desert crossing was generally considered a test of endurance, to the poetically inclined there was a certain romance to it:

Published quarterly, the P&O handbook provided would-be travellers to the 'Empire' with route maps, sailing schedules, agents' details and baggage charges.

A moonlight journey was most striking. The seemingly boundless expanse, the silence only broken by the driver and the muffled sound of the horse's feet … the whitened bones of countless troops of camels … glistening in the moonlight; then the sudden daybreak, the solitary Bedouin family mounted aloft on their desert ship.

Even when the railway came to replace the van, although travelling time was shortened considerably, the journey was still not particularly pleasant:

But such a train! Carriages of English make that had once been in order, now cracked with heat and neglect; doors that wouldn't open, windows that wouldn't shut; bunches of horsehair sticking out of the cushions, and all looking less like vehicles for active service than ancient relics.

The Suez Canal made conditions altogether easier for travellers

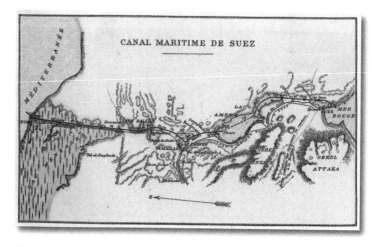

although, with an average width of just twenty-five yards, it was narrow and ships were obliged to slow down and transit by day only. In time the arrival of on-board electricity meant that the canal's banks could be lit up by the ships themselves, easing both the passage and the time it took.

Despite its obvious benefits, the very existence of the canal posed a serious threat to P&O, which was slow to adapt to the changes it brought. For one thing the company's fleet was not particularly well suited to canal travel: neither its fast, relatively small steamers to Alexandria; nor its much larger fleet running on from Suez. In addition, P&O had made considerable investments on the overland route with depots, hostelries and staging posts. The company's own resistance to change was only reinforced by the Post Office insisting that mail should continue to be carried by land. Faced, as it was, with real competition for the first time, the company was obliged to sell off many of its old, unsuitable vessels and to build up a more appropriate fleet at a considerable loss.

Anderson died the year before the canal was opened and it was left to one of his promising successors, Thomas Sutherland (at that time an assistant manager) to go about persuading the Post Office to use the canal. The young Sutherland led a charge to restore P&O to its previous glory by ordering suitable ships to be built and by developing a fleet of tramp steamers as feeders to the regular mail routes. Through these, P&O was able to extend its influence across the Indian and

Pacific Oceans to interim ports (not warranting visits from the larger ships) and new cargo markets.

Sutherland was to guide P&O for some forty-two years and, nearing eighty and retirement, it was Sutherland who set up P&O's controversial merger with the British India Steam Navigation Company (BI), whose routes complemented those of P&O.

The negotiations took place solely between Sutherland and Lord Inchcape, the Chairman of B.I., who then, as if by sleight of hand and certainly without consultation, became Managing Director of the merged companies in 1914. Although at first begrudged, Inchcape's leadership was to ensure that P&O was the major shipping line 'serving the Empire' (at least the part of it that lay in the Middle and Far East and Australasia) and was, for a time, the largest shipping company in the world.

Mail bags piled on the deck of P&O's *Chitral* which ran a fortnightly mail service to and from Australia.

A map of the company's passenger services and connections in 1866.

23

LIFE ABOARD

IT WAS ESSENTIAL for P&O to keep pace with advances in ship design as it needed to be competitive in terms of speed, reliability and economy to ensure the continuance of the mail contracts. So, gradually, from the nineteenth to the beginning of the twentieth century, wooden hulls were replaced with iron and then steel; paddles with screw propellers; coal with oil and then diesel; and candle and oil-light with electricity. All of this made travelling P&O an altogether cleaner, less hazardous, and more pleasant experience.

The early fleet provided fairly basic accommodation with shared cabins. Captain Colomb bemoaned the lack of space on a crowded steamer in 1868:

> To be doubled, trebled or quadrupled up with perfect strangers for three weeks or more in a space the size of a four-poster bedstead so as to press down the Red Sea in a temperature of 95 degrees is not ... I think, an economy of comfort.

As there was limited room in the cabin for luggage, a system was developed dividing it into 'Wanted on Voyage' and 'Not Wanted on Voyage' which was still used well into the twentieth century. A schedule of visits to the hold was organised to take out necessities and particularly for changes of clothes, with tropical pith helmets and flannels coming out and tweeds going in, by the time the Red Sea was reached.

In the early days there was often only one public room or saloon and this tended to be fairly dark and certainly hot and airless. The saloon performed a multitude of functions with one central shared table, used for eating and drinking, reading and writing, playing cards and board games.

As ships grew in size the public space was expanded and subdivided into rooms with assigned functions: for eating, reading, smoking, music and so on. When it came to interior design P&O considered their typical passenger would prefer comfort over aesthetics. Nevertheless it began to think about design developments ashore and to consider commissioning professional

Opposite:
Viceroy of India was the first P&O liner to feature an indoor swimming pool, designed in the Pompeian style.

25

Passengers
embarking the
P&O steamer
Mantua at Tilbury,
the company's
home port
from 1903.

Shared cabins
and communal
bathrooms
brought their own
hazards. W.W.
Lloyd offered the
passenger some
'board ship hints'
in *P&O Pencillings*
including 'Look
before you leap
when getting out
of the top bunk'!

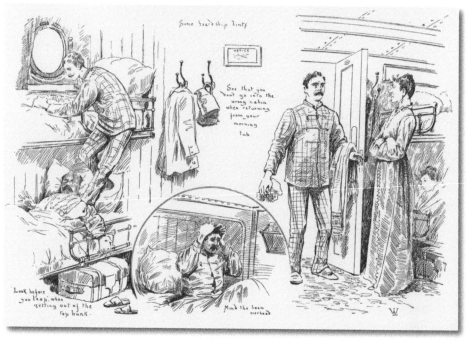

designers. High Victoriana began to creep into the fleet's furnishings. The *Himalaya*, built in 1854, had a saloon lined in maple, relieved with gilt borders and panels of glass at intervals, along with seating of crimson velvet

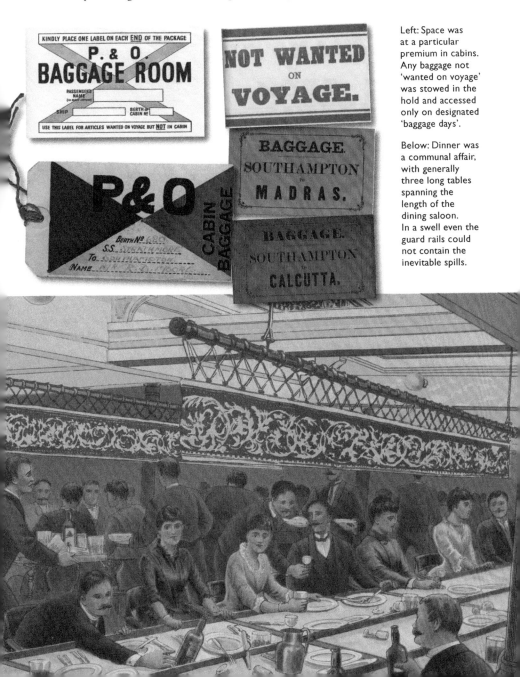

Left: Space was at a particular premium in cabins. Any baggage not 'wanted on voyage' was stowed in the hold and accessed only on designated 'baggage days'.

Below: Dinner was a communal affair, with generally three long tables spanning the length of the dining saloon. In a swell even the guard rails could not contain the inevitable spills.

Opposite:
The first-class
smoking room on
the *Viceroy of India*
designed in 1929 in
a fanciful Scottish
baronial style by
the Honourable
Elsie Mackay,
daughter of
Lord Inchcape,
Chairman of P&O.

Below: A typical
saloon on board
the *Moldavia* at
the turn of the
century. The piano
like the saloon
would be used
variously for
Sunday services
and evening
concerts and
recitals.

with gilt headings. By the Edwardian period there was not only a multitude of public rooms for different classes, but these would be linked by grand sweeping staircases topped with glass domes.

The company called upon the architect Thomas Collcutt to design some of the interiors for ships launched at the turn of the nineteenth century. Among others of their class, the *Arabia*, *Egypt* and *Persia* were all designed by Collcutt and included specially commissioned ceramic tiles by William de Morgan. Collcutt went for 'restrained' ornamentation typical of his work for the Wigmore Hall in London. Another Edwardian artist used by P&O was Gerald Moira (later to be Professor at the Royal College of Art) who provided murals.

In the 1920s P&O found a 'designer' closer to home when Lord Inchcape's daughter, the Honourable Elsie Mackay, convinced her obviously doting father of her capabilities (her only qualifications at the time being acting, the ability to drive her Rolls Royce and fly her plane!). Elsie was let loose on P&O's 'R' class of ships (following on from the 'C' class) in the early 1920s. For the *Ranchi*, *Rawalpindi*, *Ranpura* and *Rajputana* she provided interiors as showy as her own personality, and completely at odds with the Bauhaus school of simple modernism that was beginning to

sweep its way across Europe. Elsie favoured the 'historic' style with Adamesque lounges festooned with blue-and-white Wedgwood plaques, Louis XVI music rooms, Georgian pillared dining rooms and early eighteenth-century smoking rooms. Her triumphant last decorative fling

STRATHAIRD   P&O   STRATHNAVER

THE · WHITE · SISTERS

Brochure for *Strathaird* and *Strathnaver*, two of the 'White Sisters' – so called as they were the first P&O liners to adopt the company's new white livery in the 1930s.

was the resplendent *Viceroy of India*, P&O's first turbo-electric vessel. The *Viceroy*'s smoking room, which resembled an old baronial hall with suits of armour, crests, medallions and included some effects of Bonnie Prince Charlie, has gained a particular notoriety with design historians. The *Viceroy* also boasted P&O's first indoor swimming pool, in an elaborate Pompeian style.

Although P&O may have been slow to adopt 'modernism' when it came to design, they were nevertheless progressing with the essentials: electric light was introduced on the *Chusan* in 1884 and this was followed by refrigeration, radiators, and electric lifts. Air conditioning came to replace the jute sheets, the 'Punkahs', pulled by a system of ropes and pulleys by the Punkah-Wallahs. But well into the 1920s jugs of water still had to be delivered to the cabins and shared bathrooms and toilets continued to be the norm. Passengers queued, waiting their turn, and baths were filled with salt water along with a small bowl of hot fresh water to wash the salt off. In Victorian times, men would sometimes prefer to go on up on deck to catch the spray from the Lascars hosing it clean, scooting when ladies appeared lest they be caught in their nightwear. By the time the

'*Straths*' were launched for the Australian route in the 1930s, all cabins had running water, with hot and cold in first class.

The *Straths* (all five with Scottish place names) were luxurious compared with earlier ships, not only in appearance but in facilities which included a nursery, café, restaurant, lounges, reading and writing rooms, bars, a swimming pool, hospital and surgery, laundry/drying/ironing rooms, a hairdresser, a general shop, private dining rooms and a printer's shop where the daily menus and entertainment cards were produced. The *Straths* came to be known as the 'White Sisters' for they broke with P&O tradition by having an all-white hull and 'upper-works' with buff funnels and masts, compared to the previous livery of P&O ships: a black hull and buff superstructure.

It was said that there were only six occupations to indulge in by those travelling at sea: 'to eat, drink, sleep, flirt, quarrel or grumble'. Of these eating seemed to take up a good deal of time, even in the early ships. Victualling was the purser's responsibility, both at the start of the journey and along the way at stopping ports and P&O began to invest in farms along some of its routes to ensure fresh supplies.

Until refrigeration was widespread, meals largely consisted of meat, with vegetables appearing occasionally and not very attractively served. What the

The 'ironing room' in tourist class, on board P&O's *Stratheden* in 1937. With the voyage to Australia taking several weeks simple facilities for washing and ironing clothes were much needed.

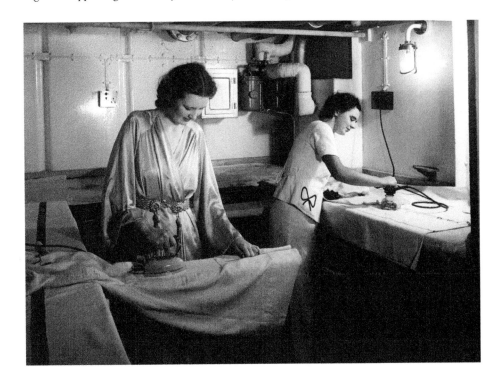

food lacked in finesse it made up for in quantity. A typical day aboard revolved around a set pattern of:

7 a.m.	tea, coffee, an orange 'in one's cabin'
8–9 a.m.	breakfast to include cold and warm meats
11 a.m.	tiffin – biscuits cheese drinks
4 p.m.	dinner – soups, roasts, fowls, pastries, puddings, cheese, fruit
7 p.m.	tea
8–10 p.m.	grog – biscuits cheese wines spirits

Daily menus were printed on board ship. Specially designed decorative souvenir menus were used for 'gala' and fancy dress evenings and included space for signatures.

Until the 1870s, P&O, unlike other lines, supplied free drinks: wine, beer, spirits and mineral water – and champagne was provided twice a week. The company was particularly renowned for the quality of its clarets (which could be sampled in the office in London).

Although eating took up a good deal of time, the ever-present threat of boredom had to be kept at bay. Even on the earliest ships, with only the one saloon, there would be singsongs to pass the time, card playing and promenading, where open decks existed. And then there was Sunday morning service taken by the captain, with all the crew in their Sunday best. A table would be dressed with the Union Jack to give some dignity to the proceedings. Typically there was a limited number of themes to the sermons: 'save us while at sea'; 'lead a moral life' (targeting the young men possibly going into temptation); 'praise the glory of the Empire'; and 'God Save our Queen, or King'. Among the passengers there was often a number of missionaries and ministers, who could, with the captain's permission, hold their own evening services. At times this race to reach the captain caused open warfare between 'high' and 'low' church.

Until the First World War, and occasionally beyond, entertainment was provided largely by the passengers organising themselves by committees. The members of these would be elected and there were more than a few ruffled

P&O   MENU

feathers on being excluded from this honour, which others found onerous. For much of the nineteenth century one committee served the purpose but, over time, they began to proliferate, spawning separate committees for dances, children, cards, debating, concerts, sweepstakes and so on. And they became increasingly formalised with the appointment of chairmen, secretaries and treasurers.

One can only be amazed at the ingenuity of the human mind in thinking up activities to fight boredom; anything that could be thrown, caught or pulled, however silly, was made into a game. Quoits and sandbags were thrown, ropes were tugged, potatoes and obstacles were raced, balls were batted, needles threaded, cigarettes lit, all in the name of entertainment. And everything was competitive: port versus starboard, passengers versus crew and even passengers versus teams ashore. Although crew were forbidden to bet, passengers gambled on practically anything that came to mind and particularly on the passage of the ship. Board games were usually chess, whist, cribbage and euchre (a trick-taking game using a pack of 24 cards).

And then there was music. At first this might only be provided by crew members who would play both in the morning and again in the evening. At least one early P&O captain 'entertained' his passengers by playing the *Messiah* on the harmonium every night. In due course passengers themselves

Following naval tradition, it fell to the captain to conduct divine service every Sunday in the 'saloon', which was adapted for the purpose by the addition of a makeshift lectern draped in the Union flag. (*P&O Pencillings* by W. W. Lloyd)

Right: A 'Daily Log' charted the progress of each voyage and was quickly seized upon by passengers as a competitive opportunity to place bets on the speed and distances covered. (*P&O Sketches in Pen & Ink* by Harry Furniss.)

Below: Deck games on board ranged from the inventive to the ridiculous but were always a great source of entertainment. (*P&O Pencillings* by W.W. Lloyd)

would put on concerts, using whatever instruments they had brought along with them and singers would perform popular parlour songs of the day.

Sightings at sea were sources of great interest and when another ship came into view a Lascar would sound a gong – one tap for starboard, two for port – so that everyone could rush to the appropriate viewing point. There was a good deal of diary-keeping and letter writing, describing views along the coastline and the ports en route, although few could better Thackeray's flowery offering:

> ... came on deck at two in the morning to see a noble full moon sinking westward and millions of the most brilliant stars shining overhead ... The view of it inspires a delight and ecstasy, an inexpressible love and reverence

At sea, a ladies' tug-of-war ensues on board the *Viceroy of India*, officiated by a number of gentlemen referees.

Right: By the 1950s the sports and entertainments on board were organised by the company rather than the passengers.

Below: In 1937 P&O marked the company's centenary with celebrations throughout its outposts including Port Said in Egypt (photographed here).

towards the Power which created the infinite universe blazing above eternal and the vast ocean shining and rolling around – fill the heart with a solemn, humble happiness.

Most passengers would go ashore at ports of call and, if loading and unloading was to take some time, take trips inland or even stay ashore overnight in some local hostelry. Tying up was usually a theatrical matter with locals rushing to take advantage of what they hoped were gullible

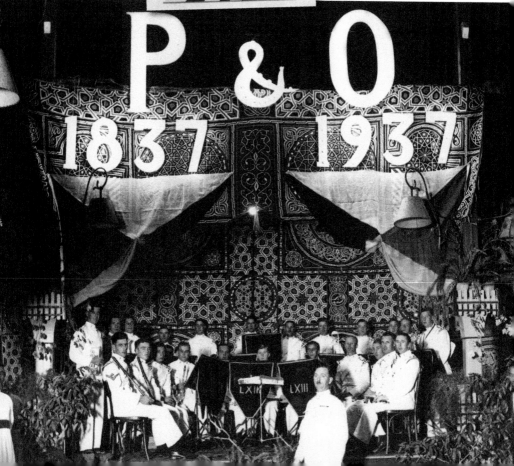

passengers. A description of a docking at Marseilles in 1901 gives something of the flavour of the spectacle:

> There ensued a scene which baffled description – young boys and girls, old men and old women on the quay, some with violins, some with harps – some playing 'God Save the King', others playing the 'Marseillaise' while others struck up the commonest music-hall ditties such as 'Daisy Bell' and the 'Washington Post', while acrobatic feats were indulged in by many, one man cleverly catching coppers on an umbrella which were thrown to him, while one poor girl poor thing stood on her head.

By the 1920s a certain amount of amateurism and silliness had gone from the entertainment, which became altogether more professional and largely provided by the company with varying degrees of success: Annie Besant (surrounded by her Theosophist followers) lecturing on 'reincarnation' might well have had passengers rushing for their deck quoits in relief. In the inter-war years 'health and beauty' was to the fore with much swimming, sun-bathing, ping-pong and doing daily the required number of trots around the deck to keep trim. There was nightly dancing to professional bands and cinema shows, but the simple pleasure of fancy dress retained its popularity (with 'Bedouins' much in favour).

An ever-popular fancy dress party in 1933.

P&O AT WAR

MANY P&O vessels, from the earliest paddle steamers onwards, were either armed with basic weaponry or, from time to time, converted into warships. This was not only when the Government needed to charter or requisition the company's mail ships but for P&O to defend its own routes, particularly in the Far East where piracy was prevalent. Even before P&O was fully established, Willcox and Anderson were embroiled in Peninsula politics, raising finance and gun-running for the Portuguese Queen faced with insurrection and aiding the Spanish Queen against the pretender, Don Carlos.

By the mid-nineteenth century the British Government could no longer rely solely on the Navy's aged officers and outdated fleet in times of conflict. Mercantile fleets and particularly those like P&O's, which were subsidised under the mail contracts, could provide much-needed additional tonnage. The company was certainly already carrying troops for the Government in the 1840s and, in a celebrated incident, a P&O steamer, *Canton*, came to the aid of a besieged naval vessel, HMS *Columbine*, under attack from pirates close to Hong Kong. On account of piracy, P&O routinely carried a supply of arms on board and guarded them with suspicion: 'In ships carrying Chinese passengers the Arms must be kept under lock and key where they are inaccessible to the Chinaman, but handy for use at a moment's notice by the officers.'

With the start of the Crimean War in 1854, P&O became involved in warfare for the first time on a significant scale. The transportation of soldiers, along with their horses and equipment, was largely carried out on P&O vessels; at times nearly one-third of the company's tonnage was so employed. P&O ships also transported the wounded back to hospitals in Scutari, and Florence Nightingale and her first group of nurses travelled out from Marseilles on P&O's *Vectis*. All told it was estimated that P&O carried some 2,000 officers, 60,000 men and 15,000 horses as well as arms and stores to the Crimea.

Of course any involvement in war caused disruption to P&O's regular services, which had to be run less frequently or occasionally abandoned

Opposite:
The P&O ship *Plassy* served as a hospital ship during the First World War and was present at the Battle of Jutland, taking 192 of the wounded aboard, some of whom are shown here. Among them are crew members from HMS *Royal Oak*, HMS *Myrtle* and HMS *Lilac*.

altogether. Such patriotism did not go unrewarded and P&O was paid reasonable rates by the Government for its ships on war service. In 1882 and 1884, when there was unrest in Egypt, P&O again acted as troop carrier. *Tanjore* was moored off Alexandria in case civilians needed to be evacuated while *Carthage* made several journeys out to the region as a hospital ship. P&O obviously had a particular interest in the conflict because of its mail route and, indeed, for a short time the Post Office was persuaded to use the Suez Canal, only to be frustrated by finding it clogged up with British troop ships.

When it came to the construction of four new 'Jubilee' ships — *Victoria*, *Britannia*, *Oceana* and *Arcadia* — in 1887, P&O decided to incorporate gun platforms in their design to allow for rapid conversion to armed merchant cruisers and take advantage of a Government subsidy (which ran until 1905). More conflicts followed and at the end of the century P&O found itself repeatedly in demand: for the Ashanti expedition of 1895, the Boxer Rebellion in China in 1900 and, to a greater extent, for the Boer War (1899–1902). During this conflict the company's ships carried some 150,000 troops to South Africa from all over the Empire, repatriated the British wounded and transported Boer prisoners-of-war.

In the First World War at least two-thirds of the P&O fleet was commandeered together with volunteer crews who chose to serve in their requisitioned ships now commanded by the Royal Navy. Not infrequently this meant loss of rank with P&O captains prepared to act as navigating officers

P&O's *Canton* coming to the aid of HMS *Columbine* beset by pirates in the China Seas in 1849. (Painted in oils by Norman Wilkinson.)

Himalaya departing Plymouth Sound carrying troops for the Crimea as one of eight company ships requisitioned for the campaign. Florence Nightingale and her nurses travelled with P&O as far as Constantinople.

under naval commanders. Company ships were active in carrying troops, defending trade routes, blockading German waters and serving as hospital ships. With the development of submarines armed with torpedoes and more sophisticated mines being laid in established shipping lanes, P&O vessels faced new hazards. The strict emergency drills, which had daily proved tedious to passengers in peacetime, now paid off in wartime. When P&O's *Mongolia* was torpedoed near Bombay and sank in thirteen minutes, lady passengers were said to have taken to the boats 'chatting and laughing as if starting for a picnic.'

Not counting the losses of P&O's subsidiary companies, the company lost over eighty ships. The most tragic was the sinking of the *Persia* on a regular line voyage in the Mediterranean, in which 335 lives were lost and those who could save themselves, including the 2nd Baron Montagu of Beaulieu, survived by clinging to a lifeboat (with over twenty other people) for some thirty hours without food or water.

In spite of a denuded fleet P&O managed to keep the mail service to its regular schedule for most of the war. Lord Inchcape proudly declared to the shareholders in 1915:

> Week after week with unfailing regularity, without exception all through these sixteen months of war, the P&O mail steamers have started on their voyages from this country to the far ends of the earth with the usual complement of passengers, just as in times of peace.

Behind the scenes Inchcape was working to see that P&O should not lose out by its wartime contribution. He began buying up other shipping lines,

In 1914 P&O acquired B.I. and together both companies provided tonnage for the war effort. B.I.'s *Carpentaria*, seen here in her rudimentary dazzle camouflage, narrowly missed being torpedoed in the English Channel in 1917.

most notably the New Zealand Shipping Company, the Union Steam Ship Company of New Zealand, the Federal Steam Navigation Company, the Hain Steamship Company and James Nourse. Such acquisitions not only meant that P&O emerged from the First World War with an enlarged tonnage, but it had also extended its routes from Australia to the Americas and from India to the West Indies. By 1920 Inchcape had further added the Khedival Line and the General Steam Navigation Company and also acquired a major shareholding in the Orient Line.

In the Second World War, as in the First World War, P&O ships were rapidly converted to carry troops, to act as convoys and to carry out patrol duties. Yet again the Company's strength was that it had vessels all over the world at the start of the war and found itself in action not only in the North Sea and the Atlantic but in the Mediterranean, the Indian Ocean and as far afield as Singapore and Japan.

Many conversions of their vessels involved little more than mounting out-of-date guns on deck; and the ships, being thin-skinned, would tend to cave in on being bombed or torpedoed. A captain recorded, 'the roar of the water rushing into the torn ship was like a thousand express trains tearing through a vast tunnel.'

Life on board a troopship was, for much of the time, a waiting game. One crew member on an escort run to South Africa described the boredom being lightened by singsongs, boxing matches and Fred Astaire and Ginger Rogers' films. It was not only regular P&O crews who served during the war, but also the Chairman, Sir William Currie, who took leave of his watch to act as Director of the Liner Division of the Ministry of War Transport.

One curious little wartime activity that involved P&O was 'degaussing'. At Tilbury Docks the company installed the launch *Faun* which was fitted out

The once-magnificent liner, *Viceroy of India*, ended her days at the hands of a German U-boat. She was torpedoed off the coast of Algiers and sank a few hours later on 11 November 1942.

Strathaird as a troopship docked at Cape Town. *Strathaird* carried the first South African troops involved in the North Africa landings and repatriated troops and prisoners-of-war at the end of Second World War.

to place cables around any vessel; these, when electrified, could reverse the ship's magnetic field, making it less vulnerable to mines.

P&O losses in the Second World War were disastrous; the shipping group as a whole lost 182 vessels. The earliest and most devastating disaster was

One of P&O's armed merchant cruisers in action in the Second World War with a Kingfisher seaplane mounted on a catapult.

the sinking of the *Rawalpindi* in 1939. She was part of a fleet attempting to enforce the blockade of Germany when she was confronted by the German battle cruisers *Scharnhorst* and *Gneisenau* between the Faroe Islands and Iceland. It was a grossly uneven match, as Neville Chamberlain later acknowledged:

> Those men must have known as soon as they sighted their enemy that there was no chance for them but they had no thought of surrender. They fought their guns until they could be fought no more, and many of them went to their deaths, thereby carrying on the great traditions of the Royal Navy.

The Falkland Islands conflict required a rapid naval response augmented by Ships Taken Up From Trade (S.T.U.F.T.). Within hours requisition notices were served including one for *Uganda*. Her conversion from educational cruise ship to hospital ship took just sixty-five hours.

The 'great tradition' of which Chamberlain spoke was characteristic not just of the Royal Navy but of the Merchant Navy too. Fifty-five of those who perished on that fateful day were P&O volunteer crew.

Peace reigned for some thirty-seven years before P&O was again called upon, to assist in equipping a Falkland Islands task force. The company was quick to respond, offering a miscellany of passenger ships, ferries, a tanker and a cargo ship. At the time *Uganda* was in the middle of one of its educational cruises for school children and *Canberra* was just finishing a three-month cruise. *Elk* and *Canberra* were the first of five P&O ships to sail to the South Atlantic. Together with *Norland* all three would play a significant part in the assault landings. As a hospital ship *Uganda* cared for British and Argentine casualties, while the *Norland* took parachute regiments 'in' and ferried Argentine prisoners-of-war out to Montevideo. *Canberra* was in the thick of the action cross-decking troops for landing. P&O had provided such support that its ships were given affectionate nicknames by the troops, such as *Uganda* becoming NOSH – Naval Ocean-going Surgical Hospital (after the television series MASH).

At the end of hostilities P&O could report, with some relief, that no company personnel had been lost, nor ships damaged, during the Falklands Campaign. In financial terms too, the group neither lost nor gained but its reputation was at a high. When *Canberra* returned to Southampton some 32,000 people turned out to greet her. P&O, by its quick and efficient response to a British emergency, had become a national treasure.

The most famous of the company's Falklands fleet was *Canberra*. Known affectionately as the 'Great White Whale' for her all-too-conspicuous presence in San Carlos Bay, *Canberra* returned to a tumultuous reception at Southampton on 11 July 1982. (Oil painting by the war artist David Cobb.)

P&O
SUMMER CRUISES
NORWAY SWEDEN
DENMARK RUSSIA
Molde
Naes
Merok
Oie
Olden
Mundal
Balholmen
Gudvangen
Bergen
Tysse
Vik
Odde
FROM
LONDON & LEITH
PRO-
GRAMME
POST
FREE
PENINSULAR &
ORIENTAL
STEAM
NAVIGATION COMPY
Northumberland Av., W.C. or
122. Leadenhall St. E.C.
LONDON.
BY T.S.S. MANTUA, 11500 TONS

CRUISING

BY THE late-nineteenth century the remedial qualities of sea water and sea travel were being recommended for every kind of ailment and a number of shipping companies began to offer cruises, extolling their benefits for health and relaxation.

It has been claimed that Arthur Anderson himself was one of the first to have the idea when in 1835 he drafted a fictitious advertisement for a cruise to the Shetland Islands, the Faroes and Iceland, to fill up a 'dummy' edition of his proposed *Shetland Journal*. In 1844, and at the invitation of P&O, Thackeray travelled 'gratis' from London to Cairo on three different company ships, describing his adventure as a 'Mediterranean Cruise'. In his published account of the tour Thackeray includes a good deal of 'grumblings' but he did come up trumps with:

> It was one so easy, so charming, and I think profitable – it leaves such a store of pleasant recollections for after days, and creates so many new sources of interest – that I can't but recommend all persons who have time and means to make a similar journey ... to see the living people and their cities, and the aspect of Nature, along the famous shores of the Mediterranean.

As with Thackeray, there were doubtless other adventurous passengers or tourists on the early ships devising their own itineraries, boarding and leaving as they wished for sheer pleasure. Among them were Charles Dickens and Wilkie Collins, who took advantage of a four-day run from Genoa to Naples on board the *Valetta* in 1853. Dickens, affected by the heat, described 'Ladies and gentlemen lying discriminately on the open deck, arranged like spoons on a sideboard. No mattresses, no blankets, nothing ... We three lay together on bare planks, covered with our coats ...'

In the 1840s P&O experimented with a branch line service to the Black Sea to complement the mail services to and from Alexandria. It was an opportunity to mark territory for future mail contracts and it gave plucky passengers the possibility of a tour to such ports as Malta, Athens, Smyrna,

Opposite:
One of the earliest posters advertising the company's new service of summer cruises to the Baltic on board *Mantua* in 1910.

In 1904 P&O converted the ageing passenger mail liner, *Rome*, to a cruising yacht, renamed her *Vectis* and introduced their first programme of 'pleasure cruises'. (Front cover of an advertising brochure.)

A PLEASURE CRUISE TO THE MEDITERRANEAN

NAPLES   SICILY

CONSTAN-   THE PIRÆUS

-TINOPLE   MALTA

ALGIERS

By the Peninsular & Oriental Cruising Yacht "VECTIS"

6000 Tons
6000 H.P.

From MARSEILLES, 22nd OCTOBER, 1904.

Constantinople, Rhodes, Jaffa and Egypt and then back to England. The new route had plenty of potential, particularly for merchants in Constantinople, but P&O had to abandon it for a number of reasons, which were compounded by the outbreak of the Crimean War. It was not until 1904 that P&O refitted the ship *Rome* (originally launched in 1881), renamed her *Vectis* and advertised her as the company's first 'cruising yacht'.

Vectis of 6,000 tons and 6,000 horsepower, has been specially fitted as a yacht to carry about 150 passengers, and will be regularly employed on the Pleasure Cruises which have become popular in combining the most delightful Holiday Excursions, with the benefit of sea air, under the most luxurious conditions. No expense has been spared in adapting the *Vectis* for this purpose, and her cabin accommodation Saloons, Card, Recreation, Smoking and Photographic Rooms will be found equal in all respects to what they should be for the work in which the ship will be engaged.

A seasoned passenger, Edward Rawdin, reported on three cruises of the Mediterranean he took on *Vectis*. Although his description is somewhat prosaic it catches some of the excitement, along with the comfort that cruising on *Vectis* provided:

...there are beautiful drawing and lounge rooms, the finest smoking room we have ever seen, the dining room is splendidly situated and the meals are excellent and well served, the steward in charge Mr Dust, the most courteous of officials we have had the pleasure of meeting, the cabins are light and well ventilated and the beds most comfortable; our cabins being No.78 and 79, our neighbour, the barber Mr Sales, who is most obliging and intelligent; it was a pleasure to be shaved by him, and his shop is the largest we have ever seen on any ship. There are three dark rooms for photographers which I have found most useful. The promenade deck is very spacious, eight trips round it the mile. This splendid ship carries a crew of 196 and has accommodation for 183 passengers and a coaling capacity of 1,800 tons.

Passengers striking a rather stolid pose for a group portrait on board the cruising yacht *Vectis*.

Below: A post-war poster designed for P&O by the artist John Gilroy, who is perhaps best known for his Guiness 'toucan' adverts.

Below right: *Viceroy of India* offered a short summer season of cruising every year from her launch. In spite of the 'modernist' advertising *Viceroy* was filled with opulent interiors designed in a traditional, historicist style.

Rawdin's first Mediterranean cruise took him to Villefranche, Corsica, Sicily, Messina, Malta, Tunis, Algiers and Marseilles – much of it in snow and rain! His accounts are particularly interesting in describing in detail the problems of getting ashore by tender: 'The tug was utterly unable to make headway against the terrific seas which swept her from end to end, and at length gave up the contest, got behind the breakwater and landed us back in Tunis.' At times it could take a tug over an hour to return passengers to their ship.

In addition to *Vectis*, P&O began to use each wave of new ships for short summer season cruising, in what was traditionally the off-peak period for liners. First came the 'M' class, a series of 10,000-ton liners, and later the 'C's and 'R's. The *Ranchi* (one of the 'R' class) was designed for and employed on the Bombay service, but her maiden voyage was a 'Norwegian cruise' in 1925. An early *Ranchi* passenger felt that such a splendid experience should only be reserved for the elite: 'no man should be booked unless he could show that he was a member of a good London club and no lady should be accepted unless she had been presented at court.' But 'cruising' by its nature introduced an air of informality and with the arrival of 'tourist class' in the

Private Sitting Room of Viceregal Suite

P&O 'Straths' were the height of modern luxury and comfort on the Australian run. In first class the Viceregal Suite with its private sitting room was a far cry from the P&O of a century ago.

1930s there was a gradual democratisation in process which would eventually lead to one-class ships.

The 'S' class 'Straths' were of particular importance in the development of P&O's cruises and it is possible that their frequent use for cruising in Australian waters from 1932, altered P&O's rather staid attitude to both class and design. The five 'Straths', launched from 1931 to 1938, were all two-class liners – First and Tourist – and brought with them an air of 'stylishness'. The interiors were more restrained than the opulent and showy Viceroy of India and breathed in at least a whiff of the freshness of modernism, albeit falling short of Orient Line's functionally designed fleet, which Colin Anderson introduced over the same period.

The brochure, accompanying the launch of the Strathnaver and the Strathaird not only waxed lyrically of their 'de-luxe suites with private bathrooms' and the 'elegant arrangements' of the public rooms, but described, in somewhat baffling detail (for the would-be cruisers seeking an idle, undemanding trip) their turbo-electric performance:

> Six mighty water-tube boilers supply the main turbines with steam at a pressure of 425lbs to the square inch and at a temperature of 725 Fahrenheit. On trial over the measured mile the Strathnaver, with twin screws exerting 28,000 horse-power, developed a speed of 23.1 knots an hour. Running at this speed, her turbo-electric machinery proved its capacity to reverse in 30 seconds.

Map showing P&O's cruises planned for the year 1939, stretching as far north as North Cape and south to the Canary Islands. Although essential line voyages continued during the Second World War cruising was halted for over a decade.

In the 1930s P&O introduced a new class of passage – 'tourist class'. Not only did it sound preferable to second class but it appealed to the pleasure cruisers.

As well as the new vessels, older ships in the fleet, including the *Moldavia* and *Mongolia*, embraced the new tourist class. In 1932 the *Mongolia* was offering 'cheap' fortnightly cruises of the Mediterranean. One John Rawdon, a local government officer from Middlesbrough, took up the offer, describing his cruise in earthy terms, focusing on the many opportunities it provided for imbibing: adjourning to the bar for night-caps, taking brandy for sea-sickness, and partaking of 'native' drinks at every port of call! But Rawdon had perceptive remarks to make on the effect that cruising had on his fellow passengers: 'a noticeable

feature is that the middle-aged are got up to look much younger than they will own up to. The younger element too look younger still.'

Rawdon's account, as Edward Rawdin's on the *Vectis*, reiterated the problems of getting from ship to shore and back: 'we left in the ship's boats, one boat lashed on each side of a pinnace. This arrangement proved very

With peace restored summer cruising was back. In the post-war period P&O launched four new passenger liners, among them *Himalaya*, which entered service in 1949.

53

unfortunate for a number of the ladies as a heavy wash was caused and thus drenched many of the passengers.'

Another entry gives a jolly account of the excitement of the fancy dress competitions, which were a feature of both regular line voyages and cruises:

> There is to be a Fancy Dress dance tonight and all the ladies are busy making costumes, mainly of paper. Special prizes are to be given for dresses made on the ship. The prizes were presented by the Commander who was fully occupied for an hour in judging the costumes. There were over 200 entrants and the most striking was a tableau representing a bull-fight complete with bull. This item caused roars of laughter and kept the crowd in a merry mood. After the judging there was a parade round the ship ...

Cruising became more important to the business of P&O after the Second World War. The regular mail contracts which had sustained and subsidised the company for so long came to an end in 1945, and faced with a rapidly disbanding Empire and promise of air travel, line voyages were also under threat. When P&O advertised their first post-war cruises to the Mediterranean the leisure-starved public applied in their droves – some 12,000 applicants in all for 5,000 berths. Increasing improvements in holiday leave and pay added to the numbers and by 1963 at least one former 'liner', *Himalaya*, was employed almost entirely on cruising duties.

A birthday supper celebrated during a Mediterranean cruise on board *Himalaya*.

The clever court cabin arrangement on *Canberra* meant that even the 'inside' cabins were afforded a glimpse of the sea.

Designed for the Australia run, *Canberra* was revolutionary in design and worthy of her tag line as 'the ship to shape the future'.

The *Canberra* (1961), the last great P&O liner, although designed and built for line voyages to and from Australia, spent the latter part of her career cruising. *Canberra* was one of the most excitingly designed P&O ships, at least as far as its interior was concerned. Hugh Casson, who had been Director of

Architecture for the Festival of Britain, and who was, by 1961, Professor of Interior Design at the Royal College of Art in London, headed *Canberra*'s design team. He may have had a special interest in the assignment as his parents had met on a P&O voyage to India. Casson, not entirely sure of what was needed, memoed Sir Donald Anderson, the then Chairman of P&O,

Sir Hugh Casson, who had designed the Royal Yacht *Britannia* took a lead role in the interior design of *Canberra*. The first-class Meridian Lounge typified the modernity of the new ship with its specially designed plastic tub chairs.

In 1974 *Canberra* was converted to a 'one-class ship' for cruising duties only. Her famous first-class pool was opened to all and a new era of leisure travel awaited the last of the P&O liners.

for advice. Anderson replied curtly that as to taste, decisions were to be made by Casson, although: 'There is no one better fitted than my brother Colin to guide decisions on anything on which you want a ruling ... You are responsible for choosing and Colin for authorising.' As a result, *Canberra* was not only fitted out with functional modernity (which typified Colin Anderson's Orient Line ships) but had much of the frivolity and colour of the Festival.

By the late 1960s P&O had extended its cruising operations to the west coast of America to pick up some of the lucrative American trade. The *Arcadia*, no longer occupied with line voyages, ran as a cruise ship out of San Francisco. Mrs Watts and her husband took two cruises on *Arcadia* in the 1960s: 'There is a timelessness at sea – it makes anyone under thirty terribly energetic and anyone over fifty terribly lazy.'

P&O's Spirit of London is coming to America!

Maiden Cruise Season 1973

The world's newest cruise ship

Despite her name, the *Spirit of London* was designed for the growing American market and operated from San Francisco.

In spite of being over fifty herself, Mrs Watts was clearly determined to soak up the romance of the experience on board:

> This evening we walked through a travel brochure – You know, the one where the passengers go to a cocktail party, have a gay dinner and, after coffee and liqueurs, stroll the deck under a black velvet sky studded with stars – well we did it all!

Expectations of the American tourist market led P&O to invest in a purpose-built cruise ship, introducing the *Spirit of London* in 1971. Quaintly, considering its market, the ship was launched with a 'London Bobby' and a 'Pearly Queen' and decorated with London themes from 'medieval' to the 'swinging sixties'.

In 1974 the *Spirit of London* was renamed *Sun Princess* and transferred to the operations of Princess Cruises, a major American cruise line which was acquired by P&O in the same year. The American experiment had proved a success and the company continued to invest in cruising, acquiring new ships and cruise operators right up to the millennium.

CHANGING COURSE

In 1910 P&O had acquired the Blue Anchor Line, which ran an emigrant service round the Cape and had profited from this into the 1930s. When again, after the Second World War, Australia was looking to increase its population to service its burgeoning economy, P&O became involved with the Government's assisted passage scheme, the beneficiaries of which came to be known as the 'Ten Pound Poms'. The scheme ran from 1945 to 1973 and provided P&O with steady returns.

While the emigrant trade provided a temporary boom on the liner services the company had long realised that it would need a total repositioning of all parts of its shipping operations if it was to survive in a post-war and post-empire world. From the 1960s through to the end of the century P&O began to diversify into such novel fields as oil exploration, building and construction, property development, and even aviation, with much complicated buying, selling and merging with other concerns.

As far as its shipping side was concerned, P&O having carried freight from its very beginnings now really went all out to develop this side of the business. Over some thirty years it scrapped or sold most of its conventional fleet and invested in volume freight: bulk carriers, refrigerated liners, tankers and the all-important container ships. Although remaining a shipping company the character of its make up was now very different from what it had been before the Second World War. By 1971 Ford Geddes, the Chairman, announced to the company's shareholders: 'From a long-established and hallowed tradition of liner services, passenger and cargo, we have moved into the new world of modern shipping requirements – going out to meet the world's needs in this way has also greatly strengthened P&O's position.'

By the late 1970s, although passengers were still being carried on cruisers, many others were taking advantage of P&O's diversification into roll-on/roll-off ferries; P&O Ferries operated in Orkney and the Shetlands, in the Irish Sea and across the Channel to Europe.

In 1983 Jeffrey Sterling became Chairman and with swift and determined leadership fought off a hostile takeover bid and set about rationalising the

Opposite:
P&O had acquired its first cargo ship in the 1870s. A century later the company's cargo division was at the forefront of the move to containerisation. The 1930s *Strath* names were revived for a fleet of new and renamed cargo ships. *Strathmuir* (1971) is shown here

In the 1950s and '60s the £10 assisted passage scheme attracted many thousands of emigrants every year, the great majority travelling to a new life in Australia on a P&O or Orient Liner.

£10 TAKES YOU AUSTRALIA

Australia is the land of golden sunshine, golden beaches—and golden opportunities! YOU and your family can share in Australia's growing prosperity. Under the Assisted Passage Scheme adults travel for only £10, youngsters under 19 travel free. For more information fill in the coupon below and post it NOW.

By the time the liner routes had all but ended in the 1970s, P&O had diversified into a wide range of activities – both on and off the sea and, for a time, even in the air.

company to ensure each P&O business concern was made profitable or dispensed with. And following the merger with Sterling Guarantee Trust, a new P&O era emerged.

By the time P&O celebrated its 150th anniversary in 1987 the company had mushroomed into a global conglomerate with interests in almost everything across the world: from business parks in America to supply vessels

in Antarctica. Gradually the company reconsolidated its efforts, focusing on ports, logistics and its remaining shipping concerns in containers, ferries and cruises.

In 2000 the cruise operation was demerged from P&O to form a separate company, P&O Princess Cruises Ltd., now owned by Carnival Corporation. In 2006, P&O and its ports, ferries and logistics businesses were acquired by DP World, one of the largest marine terminal operators, attracted to P&O because of its expansive portfolio of ports throughout the world.

P&O's history, perhaps more than that of any other shipping line, can be said to be one of service; even in periods when it was pre-eminent commercially, it served its country whether carrying its mail, its military or its civil servants. And P&O's most effective chairmen also contributed to their community ashore, from Anderson, Willcox and Sutherland, who all became Members of Parliament, to Jeffrey Sterling who was made a Life Peer in 1990.

To describe P&O as one of the country's most effective, and often glamorous, British workhorses for some 175 years, is to give it the tribute it deserves.

The *Spirit of Britain*, the first of two new ferries operated by P&O Ferries on the short sea crossing between Dover and Calais.